JAYSON TATUM

THE STORY OF HOW JAYSON TATUM BECAME ONE OF THE NBA'S MOST EXPLOSIVE PLAYERS

By

JACKSON CARTER

Copyright © 2021

TABLE OF CONTENTS

LEGAL NOTES

Jayson Tatum is meant for entertainment and educational use only. All attempts have been made to present factual information in an unbiased context.

"An NBA Player"

When Jayson Tatum was just a first-grade student, his teacher asked him what he wanted to be when he grew up. The youngster answered matter-of-factly, "An NBA player." Did his teacher readily support his dream? "Pick a realistic profession, please," she quipped. But Jayson's single mom didn't let that teacher rest on her laurels for long.

"I was livid," Brandy Cole recalls. "I went into the school the next day and talked to the teacher, and it wasn't a two-way conversation. I said, 'Ma'am, with all due respect, if you ask him a question and he answers, I don't think it's appropriate to tell him that's something he can't achieve when I'm at home telling him anything he can dream is possible.'" Tatum and his mom may have struggled a bit then. But now, Jayson is a high-flying Celtic, cruising through the rarified NBA stratosphere, focused on finding a way to get Boston past their nemesis, the L.A. Lakers.

GROWING UP IN THE TATUM HOUSE

Jayson was born on March 3, 1998 in St. Louis, Missouri when his mom was still but a teen. In fact, Brandy was on the verge of going to college when she suddenly learned she was pregnant. Should she drop out of school to have her baby? The single mom gave birth to a bouncing baby boy, Jayson, during her spring break and went back to class the following week. She continued to bring Tatum the toddler to class, including college, law school, and finally business school.

Once, when his mother was cracking the books in law school, she recalls Jayson lying at the foot of the bed leafing through a few of her texts on property law. "Mom, I don't want to ever read these kinds of books," he quipped. "I want to play basketball." The mother answered, "Well, you better work really hard." Indeed, their lives up to that moment had been seriously hard. Cole had taken Tatum out of her own mother's house when he was only six months old—she craved independence and a life they could call their own.

She managed to buy a minuscule two-bedroom house that measured 900 square feet in a diverse

St. Louis neighborhood known as "University City". The house even had a backyard, although it was surely skimpy, and a chain-link fence. One particular day, Cole picked up her young son at school and when they arrived at home, Jayson saw a bright pink paper slip attached to the door. The house was foreclosed.

"And she started crying," Tatum recalled. "I didn't know what to do. I just felt helpless. I wanted to help so badly. But I was just 11 years old." Cole looked sorrowfully at her son, with tears streaming down, and promised, "All right. I'll figure something out. I always do."

There were lots more tough times to come. Bills went unpaid for months; now and then, the utilities were turned off. For a few years, Jayson slept in the same bed as his mother. There was even a period when they didn't have any furniture at all. But the hard work paid off for both mother and son.

Tatum's high school coach at Chaminade College Preparatory School in Creve Coeur, Frank Bennett, later recalled Jayson's budding work ethic: "I get to school at about 6:30 every day and he would be here at 5:45, 6 o'clock at the latest getting his work in. What's impressive is that he did it every... single... day! I remember the only day he took off. It was the day after we won the state championship. That was his only day off. That is just him. He just worked and worked and worked and worked."

Though Jayson's parents weren't married, his dad was definitely still around. Tatum's father, Justin, recalls precisely the moment he realized that his son had a special talent when it comes to basketball. Tatum was in the fifth grade (11 years old) and playing with adult men in a league—and he was averaging some 25 points per game. "The older guys were like, 'Hold on, how old is this kid?'" the elder Tatum chuckled.

Tatum's mom was the one who raised him through thick and thin, but his dad made sure to call his son every day. Much earlier, Tatum had toddled around his dad's locker room at Saint Louis University, listening to pre-game speeches by passionate coaches, with his eyes wide in amazement. Justin got the chance to play professionally in the Netherlands and his mother took him abroad to visit his dad. By the time Justin's international basketball career was over, he came back to St. Louis and was happy to become one of Tatum's primary coaches. That's not to say that the constant coaching, caustic criticism, and tough training were easy on the youthful Tatum. "My dad coached at Soldan (International School) for like six years. So when I was in fourth grade, until like 9th or 10th grade, I used to practice with him four to five times a week," Jayson said.

For Jayson, the practices were basically brutal. Everyone knew he was the coach's son and his mistakes always stood out. He was often made an example in front of the other kids and had to shoulder more responsibility (and blame) than most of the kids. Maybe that's one reason why Tatum's shoulders are so massive now that he's blocking, dunking, and lighting it up for the Celtics on the world basketball stage.

"He was like the meanest person ever when I was growing up," Jayson jested, recollecting the times he spent with his dad as a pre-teen and teenager. "If I messed up, he was harder on me than he was on the other kids. I used to cry every day. I used to basically almost quit basketball every day because of him."

Justin joked right back: "I was like, 'Man, you're light-skinned, so you've got to come in here and be tough.'" But the rising star now says he's grateful to his dad. Those laborious lessons and long sweaty sessions were exactly what the doctor ordered.

Jayson needed someone to stick by him and at the same time challenge him to move above and beyond his capacity. In hindsight, this is something he would never change. "He saw the potential in me before I saw it in myself, so having him be that tough on me in basketball really, you know, made me tougher on and off the court," Jayson admitted.

Justin insisted he knew that if his son could tolerate the tough climate at Soldan, he could manage anything life threw his way. This referred to all things beyond the four lines of a basketball court. "He got a good look at the overall culture of St. Louis," Justin claimed. "We didn't want to shelter him from anything that was real."

Jayson isn't afraid to admit that he's witnessed his fair share of the good, the bad, and the ugly in the big city. He continued by saying that many people just don't realize what it's like for kids trying to grow up in specific neighborhoods and still stay focused. This was the reason why he let his persuasive words be heard in view of the recent racial struggles and tragedies in the United States of America.

At the end of the day, Jayson's connection with his dad is almost as much like a friendship as a father-son relationship since they're relatively close in age. Justin made sure that his son knew everything about rappers from his generation, such as Jay Z, Tupac, and Biggie. On the other hand, Tatum taught his dad which sneakers were hip at any given moment. When Tatum made it to high school, he'd even loan his shoes to his dad. Tatum's feet were a size bigger, so his dad made do with extra socks.

However, if you quiz Tatum on where he picked up his confident and mature behavior, he'll make sure you know it's all down to his mom. "I'm the biggest mama's boy ever, and I'm proud to say it," the youngster admitted then. Whenever he was home, his mother drilled and grilled him. Tatum would be kicking back, playing NBA2K in his room, but his mom would barge in and tell him to stop the game. And the next thing she'd do was thrust a comb or hairbrush in front of his face. It was meant to be an imaginary Mike.

While taking a break from her legal career handling prickly policy and compliance issues, she'd quickly take on the role of the interviewer. Naturally, Jayson was the star player. She'd start by asking him all about the video game as if she was someone like Craig Sager, the buoyant TV announcer with the outrageous suits. "Who's going to ask me these questions, ma?" Jayson wanted to hear. Her simple answer: "ESPN—when you become one of the best players in the country."

But Brady wasn't ever the kind of mom who just wanted to see her son put the ball in the hoop. According to something Jayson later wrote: "Whatever I was doing off the court, she said, was just as important as the numbers I was putting up on the court. In addition to homework, Mom got me involved in volunteer work helping out at a homeless shelter and mentoring young student-athletes in our city. I would go to their practices and games and talk to them about problems they were facing in school. Sometimes I would get to speak at their banquets or other team functions." Whatever happens in Jayson's basketball career in the future, he will always have his voice, and his mother made sure he would vocalize his feelings and understanding from an early age.

Just so you know, Jayson is also a big brother. He has two younger siblings—brother Jaycob who turned 15 in 2020 and little sister Kayden who turned eight—both from father Justin's other relationships. The elder Tatum informed the St. Louis Curator that Jayson is "head over heels in love" with Kayden and dedicated some of his high school game performances to her.

In the same interview, Justin claimed that he wanted to be a major part of their lives because he wasn't around too much during Jayson's childhood. "I want to be dominant in their lives," Justin asserted in 2015. "I thought, whenever I have a son or a daughter, you will always know me for the rest of your life, and I will do whatever I can to help you. That's what I've learned the most because this is my heart," he continued. "It would stop beating if I don't see them."

Gaining National Prominence

Tatum attended Chaminade Prep in St. Louis in the "Show Me State" of Missouri. He can safely take credit for some of the innumerable banners that flutter in the gym rafters there. As a freshman, he racked up 13.3 points and 6.4 rebounds per game and was declared the 2013 Metro Catholic Conference Co-Player of the year. Despite his raw youth, he led the Red Devils to both Metro Catholic Conference (MCC) and Missouri District 2 titles.

As a sophomore in 2014, he boosted his averages to 26.0 points and 11.0 rebounds per game, while claiming second-team Naismith Trophy All-American honors. An action video clip from his sophomore season, no less, has been viewed in excess of 40,000 times. Tatum continued to ramp it up as a high school junior in 2015, averaging 25.9 points, 11.7 rebounds, and 3.4 assists per game.

In the summer after his junior season, Tatum joined the St. Louis Eagles Amateur Athletic Union (AAU) squad, which played in the extremely competitive Nike Elite Youth Basketball

League (EYBL). In a game on July 11, the Eagles and Tatum took down future Duke running mate, Harry Giles, and Team CP3, 74-73, in the Nike Peach Jam Semi-Finals. Jayson chipped in with a game-winning buzzer-beater, arguably the most critical of his 28 points and five rebounds in the contest, to march on to the championship final.

On July 12, after a few hours' rest, Tatum scored 24 more points, grabbed seven rebounds, and rejected four shots in a 104-77 loss to the Georgia Stars and another future ringer for Duke, "one-and-done" Wendell Carter Jr. (who ended up with the Chicago Bulls), in the 2015 Nike Peach Jam championship game. During the circuit, Tatum soared above his EYBL peers, leading in scoring with 26.5 points and averaged 9.5 rebounds per game.

Prior to his senior year, Tatum made a verbal commitment to play with the Duke University Blue Devils and Coach K, turning down the North Carolina Tar Heels, the Kentucky Wildcats, as well as his mom and dad's alma mater, hometown

Saint Louis University, and the ever-lucky "Billikens".

Why did Jayson choose not to follow in his father's footsteps and enroll at St. Louis? No, it's not because his dad's feet were a size and sock smaller. What was the real deal at Duke? Tatum recently explained why the Blue Devils are at a different level when compared to other elite programs. "It really is like a brotherhood," Tatum proclaimed during Episode 4 of "The Old Man and the Three" podcast with 14th-year NBA vet and former Duke guard, J.J. Redick.

"I feel like they came up with that name a few years before I got there. Just the connection that we all have, whether you're 10, 15, 20 years apart from one another—we've all seen each other play, rooting for one another. Any time you see somebody or interact with somebody that went to Duke or played at Duke, there's always a bond, some type of connection. That's really special," Tatum concluded.

And what is it about this "crazy" guy glaring at players from the Duke bench; the one they call Coach K because his last name is too difficult to say and write? "I tell people all the time that the most important part is that we all played for the same coach (Mike Krzyewski). A lot of other programs can't say that. All of us played for Coach K. I think that's what separates us," Tatum added.

It turns out that Coach K is indeed the winningest coach in NCAA Division I men's basketball history. He's nabbed four national championships, 12 ACC regular-season championships, 15 ACC Tournament championships, 957 wins, and probably still has a few more years of coaching ahead. Krzyzewski will undoubtedly conclude his career as one of the grandest coaches in the history of all sports. Coach K became the head coach at Duke in 1980 after a stint coaching at Army, and he's proceeded to make the basketball program into a legendary, practically unbeatable force.

Players who commit to playing for Coach K at Duke receive abundant amounts of exposure, adoration, and criticism. Does this environment sound anything like what Tatum endured with his dad at Soldan? In order to thrive in those particular surroundings, Coach K has to be very careful about the players he brings down to Durham, N.C.

In short, the Duke coach is adamant that his top recruits demonstrate the following five characteristics: Embrace the "family culture", be coachable (partially a reflection of the coaching Mike himself received from the iconic Bobby Knight while he was at the U.S. Military Academy in West Point), have "high" character (including staying out of trouble and succeeding after moving on from the program), be intelligent and meet success in the classroom (which is necessary when you attend a university ranked 8th in the country in academics), and finally, possess exceptional talent on the basketball court.

As with most top athletes, Tatum didn't spend a lot of time on the leafy Duke campus being wooed. "I only took one official visit when I was in high school. They played Syracuse. I was there for a weekend, got to go to practice, go to a game, spent time with the team... They all would run through a wall for Coach K. They had so much love for him. I was sold immediately. I wanted to commit when I was there. My mom and dad were like, 'You only took one visit. You're only a junior in high school. Give the other schools a chance.' I knew where I wanted to go," Jayson gushed.

At one point, before deciding definitively on Duke, Jayson narrowed his Top-10 list to Arizona, Connecticut, Duke, Illinois, Kansas, Kentucky, Missouri, North Carolina, Saint Louis, and Wake Forest. He would soon cut that number by half with the aim of committing to one before November 2016.

Tar Heel coach, Roy Williams, attended several of his games, and Coach K declared him a "special player". The biggest names in basketball wanted Jayson in their jerseys, and the pull to go to an elite program was super strong. However, just spending a few minutes at one of Jayson's Chaminade games showed that his hometown St. Louis was trying to tug back just as hard.

It's important to remember briefly that Justin, Jayson's dad, was a basketball standout at Christian Brothers College High School (CBC) in St. Louis. He then suited up for Saint Louis University (SLU), along with his best friend from high school, Larry Hughes, who was later chosen as the eighth pick by the 76ers in the 1998 NBA Draft and played for eight different NBA franchises in a 14-year career.

Recall also that Brandy Cole, Jayson's mom, had just graduated from University City High when she found out she was pregnant, and she and Justin were already done as a couple. Cole already declined both volleyball and academic scholarship offers at the University of Tennessee, among other colleges, choosing a low-cost education at the University of Missouri-St. Louis, and then employing what precious little savings she had for baby Tatum's daycare and car insurance.

At the time of Tatum's birth in early 1998, Saint Louis University, Justin, and Larry were prepping to play in the NCAA tournament, affectionately known as "March Madness". The Billikens squeaked past the University of Massachusetts Minutemen in the first round and then were promptly trounced by Kentucky, 88-61, in the second round.

However, Jayson's mother, Brandy, had total responsibility for the toddler in his infancy, so his first memories of basketball weren't really formed watching his dad. Rather, he remembers playing aquatic "small ball" by himself. "We had a suction cup basketball hoop on the wall (of the bathtub), and I would shoot for hours," Jayson reveals. "I think I was pretty good at that."

Jayson made it beyond the bathtub, got into YMCA ball, and "graduated" to pickup games with his dad and high-flying pal, Larry Hughes. After returning in 2006 from a short stint as a pro in Holland, Justin coached Jayson at the age of 14 in AAU. Jayson kept growing all the while and insisted that he grow his skills simultaneously, focusing on handling the ball and working the perimeter of the court. Finally, the summer before heading off to high school, Jayson was viewed as one of the nation's top eighth-grade hotshots.

He also appeared to be entering the perfect prep school. Chaminade produced standout Bradley Beal as well, a longtime friend of the Tatum family who went on to play with the Washington Wizards, along with the Golden State Warrior forward, David Lee. Then, as it happened in 2013, Justin earned the coveted coaching job at his beloved alma mater, CBC.

Once, he'd actually dreamed of putting his own son into the CBC starting five, but transferring schools meant Jayson had to sit out one year. As a result, the dad and his boy suddenly became heated rivals. In the end, Jayson's team won three out of the four games the two schools played during his time at Chaminade. But Justin had hoped to see Jayson play at his college alma mater despite the heavy hands of the elite of the elite, none other than Duke and North Carolina.

Of course, Jayson had always been all ears when the tall tales of Justin and Larry's era at SLU were told again and again. That was truly the golden era when record crowds packed the Scottrade Center, all dressed in Billiken blue. Both Justin and Hughes were initially bound to play college hoops out of state, but when Hughes's brother's heart condition took a turn for the worse, they decided to commit to the local Billikens and to "Spoonball".

That was the name given to former SLU coach, Charlie Spoonhour's specific style of play. And what exactly was the coach's preferred style? Scott Highmark, a star in the mid-1990s under

Spoonhour at St. Louis, remarked, "Coach Spoon always wanted us to have fun. When he came here, the tone was pretty negative. But he said to (Erwin) Claggett and me, 'We're just going to have fun. This is not like life and death.'"

However, Justin had come to the realization that SLU no longer had that certain hoops seal of approval and that Jayson's buddies at USA Basketball would never understand the attraction of hometown Saint Louis. If Jayson somehow decided to sign with a Missouri school, Justin mused, it might have become a popular destination. "Be a trendsetter," Justin stressed to his son. "You don't have to go on this road because it was made for Shane Battier or Grant Hill. You can do what they did—at home."

Making a Decision

In the meantime, Jayson was also pulled in by the allure of USA basketball and the international exposure it brought. When he wasn't yet 17, Tatum was picked as a member of the 2014 USA U17 World Championship team that secured a 7-0 record while grabbing gold at the FIBA U17 World Championship for Men in Dubai, United Arab Emirates. Jayson started in three of the seven games, averaging 11.3 ppg, 3.1 rpg, and 1.9 steals.

The following year, he continued to hoop it internationally as a member of the 2015 USA Basketball U19 National Team that won gold with a flawless 7-0 mark at the 2015 FIBA U19 World Championship in Heraklion, Greece. Jayson featured in all games, finishing third on the squad with 13.9 ppg, 2.1 rpg, and 1.9 spg, while connecting at a 48.8% clip from the field, 40% from three-point range, and 64.3% from the charity stripe.

Back home in old "Saint Lou", Justin's friend, Hughes, invariably stuck up for SLU as well. However, like he did with his constructive criticism of Jayson's games back in the day, he made sure to channel his views through Justin. Hughes, who later got into running a fitness club in Atlanta, recalls the great variety of voices that were in his ear when he was just 17 years of age. "I always preach home," Hughes admitted just around the time Jayson made the leap for faraway Duke.

Unfortunately, in terms of more recent college hoop success, home had plenty of detractors and drawbacks. Missouri and SLU were a combined 20-44 back in 2014-15, crucial years in Jayson's recruitment. Kim Anderson, who previously manned the reins at Division-2 Central Missouri, was the Tigers' third coach in only five years. Meanwhile, at SLU, Jim Crews took charge after Rick Majerus in 2012 and promptly lost to Duquesne in the first round of the Atlantic 10 tournament.

At the same time, neither local college coach seemed to be as committed to recruiting Jayson as dad Justin would have liked. When coaches came from far afield to see Jayson's high school games, while Anderson and Crews were nowhere to be seen, Jayson apparently paid attention.

In the end, Justin and Cole both told the fast-growing Tatum to go where he felt most comfortable. Corey Tate, another of Jayson's AAU coaches and a former guard at SLU, also said he had a hunch that the highly-recruited teen would make an unorthodox choice, and maybe even shock the basketball world.

Jayson already knew that one delicious thing he'd have to leave behind if he headed out of the city and state where he grew up would be the local pizza. "Thin crust, provolone cheese, marinara sauce—it's just a St. Louis thing. That's what I grew up eating," he said dreamily.

When Tatum mentioned that St.-Louis-style pizza, specifically from a pizzeria called Imo's, was his favorite food before the 2017 NBA Draft, the internet was all abuzz. Half of the comments were from those unfortunate enough to never have heard of Imo's, while the other half "complained" of the cracker-thin crust and heaps of cheese.

Back to his senior year in Missouri, Tatum wrapped up his prep career by averaging 29.6 points and 9.1 rebounds a game. In 2016, he was named the national Gatorade Player of the Year and was also selected as a McDonald's All-American, winning the Skills Competition as part of the overall event.

Among his senior-year highlights were a 40-point, 17-rebound game in a 76-57 romp over Bentonville High School and its star, Malik Monk (drafted by the Charlotte Hornets), and a 46-point explosion against Huntington Prep and Miles Bridges (selected by the L.A. Clippers and later shipped to Charlotte) at the Cancer Research Classic.

Another of Tatum's most terrific high school performances was a 40-point outburst against 2017 No. 1 overall pick in the NBA Draft, Markelle Fultz (who went on to play for the Philly 76ers and Orlando Magic), and DeMatha Catholic High School in the 2016 HoopHall Classic.

Tatum obviously enjoyed being a high school senior, posting six 40-point games all told while leading Chaminade to its second Missouri Class 5A state championship. On March 30, 2016, in the All-Star Game in Chicago's United Center, he led the East squad by scoring 18 points with eight rebounds in a 114-107 loss. In April, Tatum played in the Jordan Brand Classic (named after a certain high-flying Bull of the past), notching 18 points in a 131-117 win against the West.

What of Jayson's rating as he left high school behind for greener pastures at Duke? Tatum was rated a five-star recruit while being considered one of the best prospects in the class of 2016. He was ranked overall as the No. 3 recruit behind only Harry Giles and Josh Jackson (who headed off to play with the University of Kansas Jayhawks), and the No. 2 "small" forward in the 2016 class of high school hoopsters.

In fact, he wasn't really so small anymore, pushing the bar to 6 feet 8 inches (2.03 m.) tall, and tipping the scales at a svelte 205 pounds (93 kg) just before he went off to become a Blue Devil. By the way, mom Brady was on Jayson's case to crack the books all the while during high school. After four full years, he graduated with a 3.5 GPA.

Jayson Does It at Duke

College Sports Radio's Chris Spatola and Aaron Taylor caught up with Tatum in April 2019, as he explained his life-long dream to play in the NBA. The initial plan when he first went to Duke was to stay in Durham for only a single season. But after the five-star recruit basked in college student life on the picturesque campus, he admitted that the decision to leave quickly for the NBA wasn't a cinch.

After a breakout freshman year at Duke, one of the driving forces that made Tatum think twice about a possible return for a second year in Durham was the gnawing fact that he and the Blue Devils hadn't been able to win the National Championship the first time around.

Of course, having the opportunity to play for Krzyzewski again was an added bonus. While it was a tough choice for Tatum, Coach K completely backed Jayson's desire to soar in the NBA after a single season in college. The renowned coach still tried to check up on him every so often to see how one of his many protégés was getting along at the highest level of hoops.

Unfortunately, Tatum's injured foot prevented him from playing in all of Duke's games during his first and only year at Duke. However, in the week 29 games, he did see action. He was his sensational self, averaging 16.8 points, 7.3 boards, and 2.1 dishes per game, in addition to shooting at a 45.2% clip from the floor.

The 2016-17 version of the Blue Devils turned out to be the first ever in the history of the Atlantic Coast Conference to win four games in four days to take the conference trophy. Duke cruised past Clemson, Louisville, and North Carolina, and then nipped Notre Dame in the final.

Even so, their NCAA hopes were immediately dashed after a second-round exit against the South Carolina Gamecocks, 88-81, resulting in a hard-to-swallow experience for players, coaches, and fans alike. Dominant Sindarius Thornwell poured in 24 points in the game for South Carolina and Duke was done.

Even harder to believe was that the Gamecocks had actually survived the first round against Marquette and secured their first win in the NCAA tournament in some 44 years. Tatum took some of the rap for the loss. Even though he'd turned into one of the best isolation scorers by the end of the season, he had five turnovers, a solitary assist, and fouled out close to the end of the contest.

At this point, it's time to take a step back to analyze how Tatum wound up as one of college basketball's best players heading into March Madness after his inaugural season in front of the Cameron Indoor Stadium faithful. Jayson's teammates would be quick to admit that he played exactly like the player that Duke recruited him to be: the focus of a high-powered offense.

The coaching staff would explain that it was logical for Tatum to take his time to develop. He missed the first eight games due to his injured foot and then had to adapt to the warp speed and physical nature found at the university level.

After that adjustment, he blossomed. "I don't know if anyone can have a full appreciation of what he's done, for a freshman who missed the first six weeks of the year," Blue Devils assistant coach, Jon Scheyer, stressed to USA TODAY Sports. "That time is critical. That's when you really get a feel for what you can or cannot do."

Head coach Krzyzewski emphasized that even when Tatum was given the medical green light to play, the rest of the team weren't in sync. Then there was a break for school exams. In addition, other players sustained injuries, new and old. Coach K himself was forced to have back surgery during the season, removing the coach from his customary perch on the bench for seven games. "There's about a two-month gap of preparation that any player needs, but especially a freshman needs," Krzyzewski remarked.

"He's so good and so committed, and our guys are good with him that since the beginning of January he's progressed so much. And I'm proud of him. I thought he'd be playing at this level earlier. But I'm glad he's been able to achieve the level that he's playing at during this season that he's playing college basketball," Coach K concluded.

At one point, Tatum's teammate, Luke Kennard (the frontrunner for college player of the year at one point in the season), had this to say to CBS Sports about having the freshman as his running mate: "When he has the ball in his hands, you know something good is most likely going to happen. He's a different player just because of the way he carries himself, the way he handles himself on the court. His attitude, his confidence, his cockiness. He has that swagger—whatever you want to call it."

Tatum's play in the last month of Duke's regular season put him at a distinctly higher level. In the season's last 10 games, the lanky forward boosted his averages to 19.0 points and 7.9 rebounds per game. He played well during the Atlantic Coast Conference tournament with his acceleration, pure athleticism, and a few out-of-this-world, backboard-shaking slams.

"If he's not the No. 1 pick (in the NBA Draft), I've got to see the guy who is," quipped Notre Dame head coach, Mike Brey, after Duke handled the Fighting Irish in the ACC tournament title game. "He plays with the poise and pace of an older player. They've done a great job bringing him along and putting him in situations where he can be really successful. He's an amazingly gifted guy and he has a great demeanor. He just kind of stays calm and plays."

At the end of the day, Tatum's one-and-done year at Duke was a success, albeit short-lived, and it boiled down to some simple factors. "My relationships with the Duke coaches were the best, and they made me a priority. It helps to be on a good team with a winning culture and be confident in myself."

It seems like a great player could say that about almost any winning team or program. Despite their "elitist" reputation, there was no place like Duke for Jayson nor a mentor quite like the Blue Devils' unique leader. "I love Coach K's passion to coach his players and to coach the game. I examined and watched the interaction between him and his staff, along with the players, and was impressed how hard they played."

Of course, life at Duke for Coach K is not always a bed of roses. The pressure to win is nothing short of incessant. Amidst these ever-lofty expectations, the Coach can get a little touchy, like when Oregon Duck star, Dillon Brooks, drilled a needless three-pointer to put the last nail in Duke's coffin in 2016. The Blue Devils were defeated yet again, and soundly, 82-68, in the NCAA Tournament.

In the post-game handshake line, pressing palms wasn't enough for Coach K—he launched into a full-blown lecture directed at Brooks about his lack of sportsmanship. Most recently, he harangued a student reporter for a seemingly innocent question (which happened to be the innocent student's first ever in a college press conference) as Duke lost to Louisville and fell to 5-5 early in the 2020-21 season.

Nevertheless, the early 2017 NCCA tournament loss to South Carolina stung all around. But Tatum still racked up solid stats in his one year as a Blue Devil. He was named to the ACC All-Freshman team and was also nominated for a Third-Team All-ACC selection. On the Duke squad, Tatum ranked fourth in free throws (118), rebounds (fifth), and free throw percentage (.849).

Tatum didn't only wow opposing coaches with his eye-popping numbers like Ohio State's Brey seemed to allude. He succeeded in attracting attention from numerous NBA front-office executives who talked about Tatum's draft value with USA TODAY Sports one week before the selection.

Some believed he'd be considered the No. 1 overall pick in the June draft, depending on which team landed it. Simultaneously, there was a pervading sentiment in general that the top pick would be either UCLA's Lonzo Ball or Washington's Markelle Fultz.

League rules prevent teams from discussing prospects until they have committed to entering the draft, so the executives only spoke on the guarantee of anonymity. "The talent is already there; it's oozing out of him," Duke senior forward, Amile Jefferson, commented on the freshman. "For our team, it was just about him being sharp. This last month, he's been doing an amazing job at evolving, doing much more—things like rebounding, playing really good defense, drawing two guys, and finding the open man."

A Dream Fulfilled

When Tatum was declared the Gatorade National Player of the Year in the 2016 high school hoop class, he joined a list of high-flyers, most of whom were already making waves in the NBA. Just how impressive is the list of players in question? The three winners who came directly before him—Ben Simmons (76ers), Karl-Anthony Towns (Timberwolves), and Andrew Wiggins (Warriors)— all wound up being chosen No. 1 overall in their respective NBA draft classes.

Of the last 11 GNPOY winners prior to Tatum, six became the league's No. 1 draft pick, including two-time winner, LeBron James, and Dwight Howard. Despite being considered one of the best prep players in the country (if not the world), and having a single stellar season at one of the country's best university basketball programs, or "factories", if you will, there were still doubts about Tatum's overall ability entering the 2017 NBA Draft.

Prior to the draft, pundits said what they normally say: "The draft class of 20XX (year) is loaded". In this case, they claimed that the class of 2017, in particular, was rich with wonderful wings—in other words, big tall forwards who can fill out NBA stat sheets with two of the most important stats every team craves: points and rebounds. Together with Tatum, there were wings like Jonathan Isaac (Florida State) and Josh Jackson (Kansas), and "instant-impact" players such as Josh Hart (Villanova) and Justin Jackson (North Carolina), and even a few "sleepers" like O.G. Anunoby (Indiana) and Terrance Ferguson (Australia).

Here's how Sports Illustrated described the enticing talent, Tatum, prior to the draft: "A scorer through and through, Tatum made his name as a prep star by putting the ball in the basket with the best of them and showed some growth in his lone season at Duke. He came on strong over the course of the season, helping lead Duke to an ACC tournament title and cementing his place near the top of the draft. He's a likely top-five selection."

What were Tatum's strengths at that point? Again, according to SI: "Tatum possesses one of the most NBA-ready skill sets in the draft, with some comfort scoring at all levels. He's able to create space for himself and make difficult shots when necessary, a necessity for most elite scorers in the league. He has the size to, in theory, play both forward positions and the length to be a passable defender with some added work. He's quick enough to attack bigger defenders and big enough to post up smaller ones. Tatum is also a solid rebounder. He enters the league with a solid offensive repertoire and has the potential to lead a team in scoring one day."

The real question approaching the all-important draft that can make or break struggling teams was: Did Tatum's weaknesses outweigh his strengths? The final piece of Si's analysis said this: "Although Tatum's skill set is impressive, he's not an athlete of the highest tier, which makes it tougher to draw a direct through line to NBA success.

"Tatum can fall in love with his mid-range shot at times and occasionally will take a tough look when he doesn't need to. He's developing as a passer but isn't a playmaker with the ball in his hands. And if he doesn't work on defense, it's hard to see how he'll impact the game when he isn't shooting the ball. Tatum will have to expand his game or risk being branded a one-dimensional scoring specialist," the SI report concluded.

In the words of Marc D'Amico, an on-air analyst, reporter, and digital content director for the storied Boston Celtics, in a report issued before the draft: "Jayson Tatum, at 6-foot-8 and 204 pounds, already has a great frame, and it will only fill out with more muscle and added strength as time goes on. He will be a strong physical specimen in the NBA.

"However, he does not possess elite explosiveness or athleticism to go along with his impressive build. Tatum, for now, is best suited to operate offensively in isolation, be it in the post or on the perimeter. He is very comfortable in the post where he excelled at Duke. He is not refined there and needs to add to his repertoire of moves. He is similar to Paul Pierce in that he creates space for shots with footwork, skill, and anticipation as opposed to elite athleticism and explosiveness," D'Amico concluded.

That was good for Tatum to hear. At one point later (after two years in the NBA with the Celts), he even said to ESPN, "I want to be the next Paul

Pierce. Spend my whole career here, win a championship, and have the whole city of Boston love me." But we're getting ahead of our story. How did Tatum actually end up in Beantown, a city that already owned 17 NBA titles (only recently matched by their greatest rivals, the L.A. Lakers), the perennial beast of the East, a city full of hardcore fans, and the proprietor of a peculiar wooden parquet basketball floor?

You may ask what players do while they're waiting to see where they'd end up in the draft pick (if they get drafted at all). Obviously, Tatum, his family, fans, and team of agents and handlers knew quite well that some NBA franchise was drooling to secure his services. But the waiting part can't be easy.

In May 2020, the young forward got together with Matt Barnes and Stephen Jackson on their "All The Smoke" podcast to share his draft-day experience. As it became abundantly clear that Markelle Fultz of the University of Washington was going to be the #1 pick, it was clear in Tatum's mind that he'd be drafted by the 76ers who controlled the third pick. But out of the blue, a week before the draft, Tatum received an invitation to visit the Phoenix Suns' facilities where he met with coach Earl Watson, their GM, and many of the staff.

When Tatum shot the breeze with Earl Watson (who played in the NBA for 13 seasons before settling in for a spell as the Phoenix coach in 2016), they immediately struck a chord. "Earl's my guy," Tatum related to azcentral.com. "I went to dinner with him the next day. I remember he picked me up. He had a white G-wagon (Mercedes Benz G-Class). He drove me around and showed me all of the houses where the players live. I called my family, I called my mom, and I was like, I think I want to go to Phoenix."

Tatum was enamored with the warm welcome and the camaraderie he received in Arizona long before he even came close to officially joining the team. "I'm sitting in the car and I'm like, this sounds good," Tatum recalled. "Yeah, I think I want to come here." You may recall that Jayson's quick decision to attend Duke occurred in a somewhat similar fashion. Shortly thereafter, it all unraveled for the youngster with two vital phone calls. Here's the way it went down, according to Tatum: "I get to my hotel and I'm about to fly back home (to St. Louis) for two days before I go to New York (for the draft), and my agent called me and he was like, '(Celtics GM) Danny Ainge called and said they're going to trade their pick. They're going to go to three and they want you to come to Boston the next day to work out.'"

Tatum's agent's call wasn't enough to make him quickly and completely change his mind. He'd just experienced the place where he thought he wanted to play pro hoops to start with, and he wasn't going to be so easily swayed away from it. Perhaps, there was one specific person who could talk him out of heading to the southwest. Remember that dominant Duke coach from a few pages ago? Mike Krzyzewski ended up ringing him and did his best to change his previous star's thoughts.

On the podcast, Tatum shared that Coach K had developed a great respect for the youthful Celtics coach, Brad Stevens. The latter had coached the Butler University Bulldogs for five years, taking the upstart school to the NCAA Championship game twice where they first lost a squeaker to Duke, of all teams, in 2010 and then fell to UConn a year later. At 31 years of age, the baby-faced Stevens became the third-youngest Division I coach to lead his team to 30 wins and the youngest to do so in more than half a century.

Coach K recommended that Jayson play for Stevens and his new NBA team, the Celtics. Tatum found it tough to override his former coach and agreed at least to work out with the Celts. "I used to hate Boston," Tatum admitted matter-of-factly. For a lifetime fan of Kobe Bryant (an NBA star who rose above and beyond the rest, and who'd played his entire career in the purple and gold of L.A.), that was possible to understand.

With his mind still ablaze about the possibility of playing for Phoenix in the heat of the Arizona desert, Tatum flew into chilly Boston just three days prior to the draft. However, all previous desires went out the window when he heard his name called loud and clear on draft day. It didn't really matter which team he played for, as long as it meant that he'd be playing in the NBA. "When I finally heard my name called, it was by far the best day of my life. It's what I'd been working for, for 16 years," Tatum emoted. His first-grade dream had been dramatically realized.

Boston's move to trade for Tatum was viewed by some as "controversial". Indeed, the Celtics' GM Danny Ainge had decided to deal away the team's #1 pick in the 2017 NBA Draft to the Philadelphia 76ers, hoping they would acquire another valuable draft pick to fit their scheme, and Boston could still target the player they coveted, namely Tatum.

Since he wasn't ranked quite as high as some other prospects on competing team draft boards, Tatum was still available and the Celtics selected him #3 overall on June 22, 2017, using the pick they received from Philadelphia. Tatum was Boston's second straight #3 pick for a small forward, following another up-and-coming scorer named Jaylen Brown in 2016.

"Most guys in my position don't get drafted to such a high-caliber team like the Celtics, so it makes me work harder because I have to compete and earn everything," Tatum reasoned. Indeed, he was well on his way to a high-caliber franchise that he`d once hated. **(7,730)**

Welcome To The NBA

After all the drama and excitement of being drafted as the No. 3 overall pick in the 2017 Draft, it wasn't clear at first how major of a role Tatum would play with the Celtics. He was rubbing elbows with three former All-Stars (including Al Horford and Kyrie Irving), along with an abundance of rising talent on a stacked Celtic roster. He knew he'd have to battle in order to gain significant playing time.

But when star forward Gordon Hayward was suddenly lost for the season with a nasty leg injury on Opening Night, Tatum was called on immediately to help fill the basket and the void. Though a mere 19 years old at the time, Tatum wasn't fazed and went on to make solid contributions that lasted all season.

As a first-year player, Jayson ended up starting 80 games, a team-best, and led Boston in minutes played (2,438), three-point shooting percentage (43.4%), and steals (83). He also averaged 13.9 points, five boards, 1.6 assists, and one steal per game. The rookie had more than a helping hand in the Celtics' 55 regular-season victories and the second seeding in the East in the playoffs.

His coaches, fellow players, and fans were all pleasantly surprised that Tatum was able to chip in from the start and take a role that was indeed monumental to the success of the C's. "We probably anticipated coming into the year, a guy that comes off the bench, plays 20-25 minutes a game, grows at a rate that everyone feels comfortable with. And then we just threw him to the wolves instead," coach Brad Stevens exclaimed ahead of Game 81 on April 10, 2018. "He's been able to handle it, and he's been great."

The inevitable comparison of Jayson to other illustrious Celtic rookies, such as the incomparable Bill Russell (who hauled down 19.6 rebounds per game as a rookie and eventually won 11 NBA Championships in 13 years), Tommy Heinsohn, Dave Cowens, and the practically unbeatable Larry Bird, was only favorable. The lanky St. Louis native established franchise records with 105 successful 3-point shots and a 43.4 percent clip from the three-point range (the fifth-best among rookies in NBA history).

Tatum also became the fifth rookie in NBA history and the first since hot-shooting Stephen Curry in 2009-10 to rack up 1,000+ points and shoot at least 40.0% from beyond the arc. He also found himself sixth on Boston's all-time blocks list for rookies (83) and eighth on its scoring list for rookies with 1,112 points.

Tatum was the tenth Celtic ever to be nominated for the All-Rookie First Team and the first since the selection of Paul Pierce following his breakout season in 1998-99. Then the Celtic legend Pierce himself, in a sudden fit of humility, admitted in May 2018: Tatum "is a way better player than I was as a rookie."

Even before his first campaign kicked off, Tatum showed off his skills at the 2017 NBA Summer League event in Utah, averaging 18.7 points, 9.7 rebounds, 2.3 steals, and 2.0 assists in almost 33 minutes of action. Later in Las Vegas, Tatum cranked out similar numbers, averaging 17.7 points, 8.0 rebounds, one assist, and almost one block in roughly 32 minutes of action in the three games he was permitted to play. As a result, he was placed on the All-Summer League Second

Team beside fellow rookie, Bryn Forbes, Cheick Diallo, Wayne Selden Jr., and Kyle Kuzma.

In his much-awaited NBA debut, Tatum grabbed a double-double with 14 points and 10 rebounds as the team's starting power forward despite the team suffering a 102-99 loss to the Cleveland Cavaliers. Tatum then went off for a season-high 24 points in a win over N.Y. Knicks on October 24, 2017. An early Christmas gift arrived when he was named the Eastern Conference's Rookie of The Month for December 2017.

The Celts wrapped up the season with a 55-27 record, entering the **2018 NBA Playoffs** as the Eastern Conference's second seed. In Game 1 of the first-round series against the seventh-seeded **Milwaukee Bucks**, Tatum notched a double-double with 19 points and 10 rebounds.

In Game 4 of the same series, he exceeded his playoff-high with 21 points and then surpassed it again with 22 in Game 6. The Celtics showed no fear of the deer as they ran past the Bucks in Game 7 by a score of 112–96, with Tatum gliding to 20 points.

The second-round series featured the third-seeded Philadelphia 76ers, and in Game 1, Tatum had a career-high 28 points in a 117–101 romp. He became the first Celtic rookie to score 25 or more points in a playoff game since that man Larry Bird during the 1980 NBA Playoffs, who also teed off against the Sixers.

After putting up 21 points in a Game 2 victory, Tatum became the youngest player ever to score at least 20 points in four consecutive playoff games at the age of 20 years and 61 days. In the process, he surpassed Kobe Bryant who accomplished the feat during the NBA Playoffs in 1991 at the tender age of 20 years and 272 days.

In his next outing, the youngster led the Celts with 24 points in a Game 3 overtime thriller, thus becoming the first Boston rookie to rack up 20 points in five consecutive playoff games. The Birdman let go of the previous record of four. At the conclusion of his playoff run, he paired with the inestimable Kareem Abdul-Jabbar as the only two rookies in the history of the NBA playoffs to score 20 or more points in 10 games during their respective first playoff attempts. Even Lebron

James, embroiled in the ongoing G.O.A.T. ("Greatest Of All Time") debate by fans and pundits, with his Airness, Michael Jordan, gave Tatum the nod. He's built for stardom," King James quipped.

CONTINUING TO GROW IN YEAR TWO

Jayson picked right up where he left off in his sophomore season. In the Celts' 2018-19 season opener, he scored 23 points, nine boards, and three dishes in a 105-87 defeat of their rival, the 76ers. October 20 arrived and Tatum bagged 24 points and 14 rebounds in a 103-101 nail-biter over N.Y. Knicks. He then scored 24 points and grabbed six boards in another win, 101-95, against the Oklahoma City Thunder on October 25. Come November, Jayson hit for 21 points and latched onto seven rebounds in an OT victory against the East rival Raptors, 123-116.

Come Christmas Day, and Tatum was feeling his generous self, going off for 23 points and snagging 10 rebounds as Boston beat Philly, 121-114, in overtime. Tatum tallied 25 points and seven boards as Boston beat the Cleveland Cavaliers, 103-96, on February 5. On March 6, the youthful Celt poured in 24 points, grabbed three rebounds, and dished out two assists as Boston beat Sacramento, 126-120.

Despite Tatum's titillating play in only his second year and the intermittent offensive explosions of

Kyrie Irving, the Celtics bowed out against the Milwaukee Bucks and their budding superstar, Giannis Antetokokounmpo, "the Greek Freak".

BECOMING AN ALL STAR

In his third NBA campaign, Tatum scored what was then a career-high 39 points, to go with 12 rebounds, in a 119–93 Celtics' win over the **Charlotte Hornets** on December 22, 2019. He would soon exceed that career-high with 41 points against the **New Orleans Pelicans** in a 140-105 blowout win on January 11, 2020. A few weeks later, Tatum was named an **NBA All-Star** for the first time in his career when he was selected as an Eastern Conference substitute.

In mid-February, 2020, Tatum would hit for 39 points again while playing a total of 47 minutes, spearheading Boston's 141-133 double-overtime victory against the L.A. Clippers. Soon after, he equaled his career-high with 41 points in a narrow loss to the L.A. Lakers, 114-112. Then the COVID-19 crisis came along and wreaked havoc on the world and the NBA.

Back in action, Tatum hit an unusual low, firing up 18 shots versus the Bucks and connecting on only two on July 31. He bounced back quickly in the next game, going off for 34 points on 11-for-22 shooting as the Celts dropped the Portland Trail

Blazers, 128-124, on August 2. He was promptly named to the All-NBA Third Team, another career first.

In the playoffs, which took place in the "Orlando Bubble" amidst the pandemic, the Celtics made it as far as the Conference Finals for the second time in Tatum's first three years as a pro. Boston knocked out Philly first in four straight games and then banished the defending champions, the Toronto Raptors, in seven tight games. Then the Celtics ran into Jimmy Butler and the Miami Heat. They fell in six games.

To top it off, the most replayed highlight from that Finals series had the Celts trailing by a couple of points in the waning seconds in Game 1. Tatum drove deep into the lane, flying in for the dunk with authority as he had done so many times at Duke and in his short NBA career. He was met in the stratosphere by Miami's massive athletic center with a name out of the movies—Bam Adebayo—and Jayson's potential game-tying jam was firmly rejected. Miami squeaked past the Celts, 117-114, only to be thoroughly routed by the Lakers in the Finals.

My Idol, Kobe Bryant

An awful lot has happened in the short lifespan of one Jayson Tatum. Just a few weeks after his NBA debut, the young star's son was born on December 3, 2017. The bouncing baby boy is affectionately referred to as "Deuce" by family, friends, and the Celtics' so-called nation of fans. Jayson has come full circle in such a short time and even admits that he's similar to his own dad at this moment in history.

Jayson wants his own son to be able to reflect on the year 2020 someday and know that his dad didn't hesitate to speak up for what he believed in. "Just for him to know his dad stood for something, and he was on the right side of history, and that he used his platform, used his voice for change, and for the better," Jayson mused.

The bizarre year of 2020 saw the world try to battle a deadly virus and ensuing worldwide pandemic, and the NBA and its players take on the phantoms of racism as well, speaking out against police brutality and the mistreatment of people of color in the USA and the world.

Jayson's bravery to speak out means a lot to his dad, Justin. The father stands proud while watching his son in his element, and he knows that many people are just as proud of him too. "I have no words for it; it speaks volumes," Justin enthused. "I love it. I'm here to change young men's lives when I coach and teach and things like that, and he can help change the world, so that's huge."

But no matter what else is going on in the world and what challenges the NBA players face off the court going forward, it always comes back to basketball at the end of the day. Jayson spoke again recently of his idol, Kobe Bryant, who was so abruptly taken away from this world, together with his dear daughter and several friends, in a horrific helicopter crash.

"Kobe Bryant was the reason I started playing basketball—always was and will be my favorite player of all time. I love the way he could get his shot off, his footwork down in the post, just his determination to be the best player. When I was like 4 or 5, my mom would ask me what I wanted to be when I got older. And I would just say, 'I wanna be Kobe.' She'd be like, 'You want to be in the NBA?' 'No, like, I wanna be Kobe,'" Tatum recalled.

His mother remembers it exactly the same way. Brandy Cole recalls that Jayson was always tall for his age, as the majority of NBA stars tend to be. "I remember after first grade, he was always taller than his teachers," said Cole in an interview with the St. Louis Curator. Kobe's name came up a lot in those early days and still does in conversations with Tatum. It's tough to think of a worthier idol than Bryant. But you can surely bet that there are some first-graders somewhere right now dreaming of dribbling and shining in the NBA like Jayson. And you can go right ahead and just let them dream.

MORE FROM JACKSON CARTER BIOGRAPHIES

My goal is to spark the love of reading in young adults around the world. Too often children grow up thinking they hate reading because they are forced to read material they don't care about. To counter this we offer accessible, easy to read biographies about sportspeople that will give young adults the chance to fall in love with reading.

Go to the Website Below to Join Our Community

https://mailchi.mp/7cced1339ff6/jcbcommunity

Or Find Us on Facebook at

www.facebook.com/JacksonCarterBiographies

As a Member of Our Community You Will Receive:

First Notice of Newly Published Titles

Exclusive Discounts and Offers

Influence on the Next Book Topics

Don't miss out, join today and help spread the love of reading around the world!

OTHER WORKS BY JACKSON CARTER BIOGRAPHIES

Patrick Mahomes: The Amazing Story of How Patrick Mahomes Became the MVP of the NFL

Donovan Mitchell: How Donovan Mitchell Became a Star for the Salt Lake City Jazz

Luka Doncic: The Complete Story of How Luka Doncic Became the NBA's Newest Star

The Eagle: Khabib Nurmagomedov: How Khabib Became the Top MMA Fighter and Dominated the UFC

Lamar Jackson: The Inspirational Story of How One Quarterback Redefined the Position and Became the Most Explosive Player in the NFL

Jimmy Garoppolo: The Amazing Story of How One Quarterback Climbed the Ranks to Be One of the Top Quarterbacks in the NFL

Zion Williamson: The Inspirational Story of How Zion Williamson Became the NBA's First Draft Pick

Kyler Murray: The Inspirational Story of How Kyler Murray Became the NFL's First Draft Pick

Do Your Job: The Leadership Principles that Bill Belichick and the New England Patriots Have Used to Become the Best Dynasty in the NFL

Turn Your Gaming Into a Career Through Twitch and Other Streaming Sites: How to Start, Develop and Sustain an Online Streaming Business that Makes Money

From Beginner to Pro: How to Become a Notary Public

Made in the USA
Middletown, DE
01 October 2023

39889291R00036